DEAR DANTE

Poems

Angela Alaimo O'Donnell

IRON PEN

PARACLETE PRESS
BREWSTER, MASSACHUSETTS

2024 First Printing

Dear Dante: Poems

ISBN 978-1-64060-937-2

The Iron Pen name and logo are trademarks of Paraclete Press.

Library of Congress Cataloging-in-Publication Data
Names: O'Donnell, Angela Alaimo, author.
Title: Dear Dante : poems / Angela Alaimo O'Donnell.
Description: Brewster, Massachusetts : Paraclete Press, 2024. | Summary: "O'Donnell travels with Dante as her guide through Hell, Purgatory, and Paradise. This is a love letter to Dante"-- Provided by publisher.
Identifiers: LCCN 2023046879 (print) | LCCN 2023046880 (ebook) | ISBN 9781640609372 (trade paperback)
Subjects: LCSH: Dante Alighieri, 1265-1321--Poetry. | LCGFT: Poetry.
Classification: LCC PS3615.D653 D43 2024 (print) | LCC PS3615.D653 (ebook) | DDC 811/.6--dc23/eng/20231017
LC record available at https://lccn.loc.gov/2023046879
LC ebook record available at https://lccn.loc.gov/2023046880

10 9 8 7 6 5 4 3 2 1

Published by Paraclete Press
Brewster, Massachusetts
www.paracletepress.com

Printed in the United States of America

Praise for ***Dear Dante: Poems***

"*Dear Dante* unfolds as a poetic correspondence between two poets in dialogue across space, time, and languages. Both are pilgrims striving to walk their paths to achieve the bliss of heaven, and though they are separated by centuries, they are not so different. Both interrogate themselves and their worlds while eliciting in their readers the desire to join and partake in their poetic and spiritual *camino*. Angela Alaimo O'Donnell's rare sensitivity as a reader and her technical excellence as a poet take us closer to the *Commedia* by making Dante's poetry alive and engaged with our modern world and selves."

—**Susanna Barsella**, author of *In the Light of the Angels: Angelology and Cosmology in Dante's* Divina Commedia

"What a splendid reading Angela Alaimo O'Donnell offers us here in *Dear Dante*, as she travels (poet with poet) with Dante as her guide through Hell, Purgatory, and Paradise! And the emotions O'Donnell registers in these responses to the Prince of Poets—from the deep, chilling wisdom and pity she gleans from Hell, to the tears for our human frailty, to that visceral sense of experiencing what is lost for good in our purgation, to understanding the necessity to let go of our ego-centered desires for the one thing necessary: Love. And all of this told, as with her other teacher, Flannery O'Connor, with a wit and honesty and deep insight where even words fail as we search for that One Word we hunger for."

—**Paul Mariani,** author of *Deaths and Transfigurations*, *The Mystery of It All*, and *All That Will Be New*

"This splendid homage in Dante's favorite forms reflects Angela Alaimo O'Donnell's love and passionate engagement with *The Divine Comedy*. Pondering the *Inferno* she outdoes the maestro in compassion: 'Perfection is a dream the heartless chase.' Her meditations on the *Purgatorio* reaffirm Dante, allowing that 'souls en route to God know how to sing' and she deftly catches his *Paradiso's* peace of heart 'Where desire is defeated, love comes first.' We both delight in these poems and are reawakened to the wonder of Dante."

—**Micheal O'Siadhail**, author of *The Five Quintets*

Contents

For Susanna Barsella
Friend, Colleague, Dantista

For Dante Alighieri
"Il Miglior Fabbro"

Introduction
Dante, Thee, and Me

Dear Dante began as a species of accompaniment.

To mark the much-anticipated 700th anniversary of Dante's death on September 14, 2021, I decided to honor that occasion by spending the summer before rereading his great masterpiece *The Divine Comedy* at the rate of one canto a day. Since there are exactly 100 cantos and there are very nearly 100 days of summer—and since *The Divine Comedy* is divided into three sections in much the same way that the summer is divided into three months—*Inferno, Purgatorio, and Paradiso* mapping nicely onto the unfolding of *June, July, and August*—this seemed a perfectly poetic way to spend the summer.

It was an intense experience, walking with Dante each day. Even on bright, sunny mornings, I found myself drawn into the dark world of the *Inferno*. The striking images would stay with me. Not only was Dante in my waking thoughts, but he also began entering into my dreams. He became a ghost haunting the hallways of my house as well as the corners of my mind. I was, at the outset, content to vicariously follow the course of The Pilgrim's journey from one spiritual space to another, but before long, I found myself entering into the poem as participant rather than passive observer. In the course of our daily visitations, I began talking back to Dante—and that talking took the form of poems, poems that at times channel his voice, at others engage him in conversation, and at still others challenge him on his theology and his oftentimes dark depictions of the consequences of human frailty.

As much as I admire the beauty, power, and wisdom of Dante's epic account of sin, purgation, and salvation, as a reader shaped by modernity I cannot help but take issue with some aspects of his worldview. Let's face it: the medieval Catholic world is a far cry from the modern one we inhabit. It's true that we have much in common in terms of the values we hold—one is not supposed to commit adultery, practice greed and gluttony, lie, cheat, or murder. However, we tend to look less harshly on human brokenness and imperfection, to err on the side of mercy rather than judgment. In addition, there are human behaviors that Dante considers grave sins that our contemporary culture and many contemporary Catholics and Christians do not, such as homosexuality and suicide, despite what the Catholic Church's Catechism might say. (Dante, was, of course, a deeply Catholic poet.) In addition, Dante also tends toward intolerance of other religions. The fact that he puts Mohammad in hell is enough to turn some modern readers away.

Of course, it's no surprise to us that the world has changed since 1321, when Dante completed his *Divine Comedy*. And yet, Dante has bequeathed us a vision and a vast cast of characters that enable us to see ourselves, with all our failings, our strivings, and our aspirations. He has captured what is universal in the human condition, even as he was subject to the limitations of his own time.

I had a similar response to the *Purgatorio*. While some of the purgative penance and punishment meted out squared with my modernist sense of justice, some did not. I was able to see the suffering souls Dante encountered through his eyes, through the eyes of Virgil (the great pagan poet who serves as Dante's guide along his journey), and, also, through my own. Some of the poems I wrote endorse and enlarge on Dante's vision, others challenge it, and still others reject it out of hand. In these poems, I dare to differ with Dante—an intellectual, spiritual, and artistic act that creates a space for encounter with the master poet, acknowledging a tension that isn't easily resolved.

My journey through the *Paradiso* with Dante was, perhaps, most instructive of all. Unfortunately, few people actually read the 3rd canticle of Dante's epic unless forced to, and so it holds for us a slew of surprises. It is the medieval literary equivalent of "Lucy in the Sky with Diamonds"—wildly beautiful, surreal, and almost hallucinogenic in its imagery and language. The casual, non-scholarly reader is often at a loss, trying to decipher the colossal code Dante speaks in. The fact that the poet himself acknowledges the limits of his powers of speech to convey the visions he sees doesn't help matters much. The blinded and inarticulate leading the blinded and inarticulate doesn't make for clarity, but it does make for lively poetry, both on Dante's part and (I hope and pray) my own. The poems in the *Paradiso* constitute a pilgrimage into the state of perfection and thus, a journey into the unknown.

My response to my daily dose of Dante amounts, in this collection, to 39 poems—13 devoted to each of the 3 canticles—plus an additional 3 poems that serve as prologue and epilogues. (Threes abound in *The Divine Comedy*, so why not here?) They are all formal poems, written in the forms Dante favored—the sonnet and, of course, *terza rima*, the ingenious verse form he invented to tell his haunting and compelling tale. (I confess to a single outlier here—one lone poem written in tetrameter quatrains, for which I offer no explanation. The muse wanders where she wills.) The sonnet serves as an ideal form to convey the act of pilgrimage. Each of the 14 lines corresponds to one of the 14 Stations of the Cross, each line a step along the journey as well as a station along the *Via Crucis* the pilgrim travels. In addition, *terza rima* is the perfect narrative vehicle, creating and maintaining suspense as it requires the reader (and the poet) to cast one's gaze ahead to see the action to come rather than dwell on what has taken place, the middle rhyme of each tercet foreshadowing the rhymes to come in the lines that follow.

In addition, each of my poems (with only a few exceptions) begins with an epigraph from Dante's poem, establishing the context and the source of inspiration for the poem that follows. In this way, each page of the book features a dialogue between Dante and me, a sort of mini drama, which the reader is invited to eavesdrop on. I have to acknowledge that, at first, it felt presumptuous setting my little poems beside Dante's Great Big One. But I enjoyed the proximity and the sense of intimacy with Dante, so I ignored those naysaying voices and just kept writing. The result is the book that follows.

I hope *Dear Dante* might offer you, Dear Readers, a parallel journey to Dante's, an opportunity to engage the *Divine Comedy* in a double-minded way—both on its own terms and also in contemporary terms—enabling us to appreciate the universality and the genius of the master poet and to simultaneously acknowledge the limitations of any artist who is grounded in his own milieu. I hope these poems might serve as an invitation to enter into the spirit of the Divine Comedy as we are pulled into Dante's fantastic story, but also make us aware of the ways in which we are different from Dante. This tension provides an opportunity for us to confront Dante—to place ourselves in his poem and to engage him in conversation—and to deepen our understanding of this challenging vision Dante creates.

Dear Dante is a species of accompaniment, an act of homage, a declaration of defiance, and a long love letter to Dante. It might also be read as a series of meditations that attest to how dear Dante is to us. The Commedia is our inheritance, a rich legacy left to readers by our brother poet 700 years ago. These poems are an admittedly small expression of gratitude for that grand and graced gift. *Grazie mille, Maestro.*

—Angela Alaimo O'Donnell
Fordham University

"Poems become stepping stones in one's slow pilgrimage, small Virgils leading the soul's Dante around the spiral of hell and paradise."

—**Denise Levertov**

"O light and honor of all other poets,
may my long study and the intense love
that made me search your volume serve me now."

—**Dante, *Inferno* I:82–84**

PROLOGUE

Dear Dante

A poem ought to be free to lie its way to the truth.
—John Ciardi

All poets are liars. St. Thomas says so.
Yet you choose verse to tell the truth.
We glide along on your easy *terza rima*,
each line, each hanging rhyme, pulling us
into deeper, more dangerous waters.
You can't look away, and neither can we
from the suffering shades, the pure agony
of unchanging pain for eternity. No
respite from the mind's and the body's fire.
If you hated your kind, you could not dream a
worse world than your endless Hell, a liar's
pandemonium no loving words can soothe.
Lured by your language, we blindly follow you,
pray none of the things you write comes true.

INFERNO

The Journey

When I had journeyed half of our life's way
I found myself within a shadowed forest,
for I had lost the path that does not stray.
—Inferno I:1–3

You're not the first to be so lost
and will not be the last.
You're not the first to count the cost

of being ruined, outcast
from the city that you called your own.
You might pray and fast,

but never can you go back home.
A new path lies ahead,
a life you'll have to lead alone.

And so you dream, instead,
of an imagined friend
pulled straight out of your head,

a poet who can mend
the bent and broken life you've led,
a poet who can send

you places that the small soul dreads,
the world of reckoning
with the living and with the dead,

who will teach you to sing
a song of loss and then of grace,
relieve you of your mourning,

and lead you to the face
of her you've loved so long and well,
redeem you from disgrace.
But first you'll have to go through Hell.

Dante Meets Virgil

And are you then that Virgil, the fountain
That pours so rich a stream of speech?

O light and honor of all other poets,
may my long study and intense love
that made me search your volume serve me now.

You are my master and my author.
*—**Inferno I:79–80, 82–85***

The leopard, the lion, and the she-wolf
the beasts that keep Dante from his path.
Alone in that wildness by himself,

there is no superhero he can ask
to save him from their jaws and from his fear.
They are lean and hungry. They are fast.

Yet as he nearly faints there appears
a savior whom he greets with mighty praise.
Even in his terror he is cheered,

for he knows only poetry can raise
his harrowed soul from the deep pit of grief,
speak the truth to astonish and amaze

the pilgrim who suspends his disbelief,

who follows his master, though the road be grim,

the steady voice and guiding hand reprieve

from the beasts that would devour him from
within.

Dante among the Poets

The shade is Homer, the consummate poet;
the other one is Horace, satirist;
the third is Ovid, and the last Lucan.
. . .
Soon after they had talked a while together,
they turned to me, saluting cordially;
and having witnessed this, my master smiled;

and even greater honor then was mine,
for they invited me to join their ranks–
I was the sixth among such intellects.
—***Inferno IV:88–90, 97–102***

It seems a sin to be happy in Hell,
but Dante finds a way to pull it off,
the grim news that he has to tell

less urgent now, the road less rough
when walked with poets who are gods
in his eyes. Let's face it, he is chuffed

to be embraced by them. The odds
unlikely—and, truly—slim
of meeting his heroes, his squad

of genii here. Who can blame him
for loving his moment in the sun?
Even Virgil smiles. This whim-

sey Dante's way of having fun,
a trick every poet knows,
claiming fame he's not yet won.

They all link arms and on they go,
speaking in lines of noble verse,
the six sages of sad Limbo,
one of them blessed, five cursed.

Christ in Hell

". . . I was new-entered on this state
when I beheld a Great Lord enter here;
The crown he wore a sign of victory.
He carried off the shade of our first father,
of his son Abel, and the shade of Noah,
of Moses, the obedient legislator,
of Father Abraham, David the King,
of Israel, his father and his sons,
and Rachel, she for whom he worked so long,
and many others–and he made them blessed."
—Inferno IV:52–61

What would Christ have thought of Dante's Hell?
He who forgave each sinner that he met
face to face with sorry souls who dwell

in torment, with no hope that it would ever let
up. Hard to believe the Savior would approve
of punishment eternal, He who would forget

his own sufferings, He who was moved
to heal the thief crucified by His side,
His killers, too, who knew not what they do.

His trip to Limbo, where shades abide
in Hell's anteroom, an errand of grace.
One by precious one, He pulled them aside,

progenitors of the holy human race,
and took them to heaven, where they belong.
Each with a name, each with a face

beloved of God, their years filled with long-
ing Christ ended at last. But what of the rest,
those He did not choose? It takes a strong

stomach to deny them, refuse to say yes,
to turn a deaf ear to their plaintive pleas.
He had to be sad, to see what a mess

He was leaving behind. How could He not grieve?
Though He rescued many, more were bereft.
Does he still think of those He did not retrieve?
I can't help but believe that Jesus wept.

Dante among the Lovers

When I had listened to those injured souls [Paolo & Francesca],
I bent my head and held it low until
the poet asked of me: "What are you thinking?"

When I replied my words began: "Alas,
how many gentle thoughts, how deep a longing,
had led them to the agonizing pass!"
—Inferno, V:109–114

The poetry is in the pity.
—Wilfred Owen

He moves among them like a spy
who has no knowledge of their sins,
beholds them with a human eye

and so his pity begins.
Instead of judgment he brings love.
As reason fails, mercy wins.

Though Dante knows the God above
has damned these souls for their hot lust
he can't deny the pathos of

their suffering. He knows they must
pay the price. Their fond embrace
has led them here. This cloud of dust

that whips them through the endless days
and nights of Hell won't let them rest.
Of all the diabolic ways

to punish, this might be the best
that one who tallies wrongs might mete.
Yet Dante feels no thrill, no zest

for just desserts. The balance sheet
God keeps appalls his human heart.
He faints from grief, knocked off his feet
by his own impassioned art.

On Fame

"But when you have returned to the sweet world
I pray you, recall me to men's memory."
—Inferno VI:88–89

Remember me, remember me
the lost souls say.
The fate of anonymity
worse in every way

to being known as infamous,
a sinner who has sinned.
Better to be dangerous,
better to be kin

to lying Ulysses, his tongue
forever flaming,
to gorging Ugolino, his hunger
never waning,

to Pia who was murdered,
Brunetto and his book,
Ciacco who's devoured.
Not to be forsook

nearly every soul's ambition—

except the chosen few

who crave the dim oblivion

they've earned, who are too

sunk in their affliction to care

about the world
beyond their endless nightmare

of ice and dark and cold.

Swimming with Dante

"But fix your eyes below, upon the valley,
for now we near the stream of blood where those
who injure others violently boil."

Now with our faithful escort we advanced,
along the bloodred ditch's banks
beside the piercing cries of those who boiled.
—Inferno XII:46–48, 100–102

I know this river. The river of rage.
Have stepped in it a time or two, and more.
Have felt it burn my soles. Left the shore
of sanity and love to wade its waters,
immerse myself in wrongs I could not right,
conjure violent wars I could not fight,
boil awhile in blood, my own and others'.
Anger is a pleasure. Anger is a cage
that holds the soul in bondage to its whim.
Once you've wandered in, all the brim-
stone in Hell cannot save you. No centaur
will rescue you (like lucky Dante). Forever
caught between desire and desire, you swim
until the madness leaves you again.

Dante among the Suicides

The poet waited briefly, then he said
to me: "Since he is silent, do not lose
this chance, but speak and ask
what you would know."

And I: "Do you continue; ask of him
whatever you believe I should request;
I cannot, so much pity takes my heart."
—Inferno XIII:79–84

The forest of suicides the darkest place
for Dante—and for us. The tortured face-
less, their bodies are not theirs, no saving grace
allows them to reclaim themselves. They are erased
forever, their flesh become dead wood, disgraced
for a moment's mortal error. No place
for mercy in their Maker's mind, so base
is this act in God's eyes. And, yet, encased
in Dante's chest is a heart like ours, birthplace
of love for the sinner in the face
of sin. He's learning that life is a race
none of us can win. We're all in last place.
Some of us fall, can't keep the killer pace.
Perfection is a dream the heartless chase.

Dante among the Diviners

As I inclined my head still more, I saw
that each, amazingly, appeared contorted
between the chin and where the chest begins;

They had their faces twisted toward their haunches
and found it necessary to walk backward,
because they could not see ahead of them . . .

May God so let you, reader, gather fruit
from what you read; and now think for yourself
how I could keep my face dry

when I beheld our image so nearby
and so awry that tears, down from the eyes,
bathed the buttocks, running down the cleft.
—Inferno XX:13–15, 19–24

The broken body holds a broken soul.
a truth Dante knows in his poet's bones,
his own eyes weeping, his own heart full

of pity for the lost daughters and sons
who believed the future was theirs to tell.
Their minds fat with pride, their mouths full of stones,

they lied their way to the darkness of Hell
while the fools thought they prophesied truth.
The pilgrim is chastened. He knows full well

that the poem he writes is damning proof
of his own folly; foretelling the fates
of so many sinners, he can't stay aloof

and judge those who did what he does, berate
and despise his own misguided kind.
But there's no turning back. It's way too late

to unwrite the journey. And so he finds
himself in dread places he did not expect.
Somehow he is spared, while they are consigned
to torture, souls cloven, their dear bodies cleft.

Dante & the Devil's Fart

They turned around along the left hand bank:
but first each [demon] pressed his tongue between his
teeth
as signal for their leader, Barbariccia.
And he made a trumpet of his ass.
—Inferno XXI:136–39

This Nicolas anon leet fle a fart
As greet as it had been a thunder-dent.
—Chaucer, "The Miller's Tale," 698–99

The most famous fart in poetry,
though Chaucer lays claim to that, too.
The music of Hell is earthy.
The music of pilgrimage proves
the fact of the body, no matter who
makes the journey, walks the walk.
The Devil's arse can talk.
Chaucer's lover's can, as well.
Flatulence an age-old joke
boys and poets love to tell.
Amid the fire, amid the smoke
erupts the sound and then the smell,
and then the roar of readers' laughter
here in the hellscape of disaster.

Vanni Fucci's Figs

When he had finished with his words, the thief
raised high his fists with both figs cocked and cried:
"Take that, o God; I square them off for you!"

Throughout the shadowed circles of deep Hell,
I saw no soul against God so rebel,
not even he who fell from Theban walls.
—Inferno XXV:1–3, 13–15

I'm shocked that you can still be shocked
given how much of Hell you've seen.
You disbelieve. Your soul is rocked

by Vanni Fucci, his obscene
sign performed for all eternity.
Fucci the thief, Fucci the mean

beast who stole from the sacristy,
pays for his crime, is burnt to ash,
then reassembles miraculously

only to burn again. His rash
act he pays for repeatedly
with no hope of release. His past

cannot be undone. The ugly
gesture his revenge, and brief
as that revenge may be

it's his and his alone. The thief
defies the God who tortures him
and earns himself some small relief

from punishment. This second sin
compounds the first, and it's the one
he's proudest of. It pleases him.

Revenge the only satisfaction
a man like Vanni Fucci knows.
He seeks and loves your shocked reaction,
and on his crucifixion goes.

Ugolino's Hell

"But after we had reached the fourth day, Gaddo,
throwing himself, outstretched, down at my feet,
implored me: 'Father, why do you not help me?'

And there he died; and just as you see me,
I saw the other three fall one by one
between the fifth day and the sixth; at which,
now blind, I started groping over each;

and after they were dead, I called them for
two days; then fasting had more force than grief."

When he had spoken this, with eyes awry,
again he gripped the sad skull in his teeth,
which, like a dog's, were strong down to the bone.

—Inferno XXXIII:67–78

What torment could be worse than this shade's?
Starved to death in life, he eats his fill,
a ghastly meal made of his killer's brains

forever. Forever freezing in the chill
of Hell's frozen lake. Forever doomed
to remember the way his sons were killed,

their hunger worse than his. All of them entombed
in a tower they could not escape
by Ruggieri, who is eternally consumed

by the grieving father, his mouth agape
and dripping blood even as he speaks
to Dante of his wrongs. It is too late

to undo his sins, what brought him to this bleak
terrain, another place he can't escape.
Bound to his foe, he has become a freak,

a flesh-eating monster, with each bite he takes
a chunk of meat and his dark revenge,
for his own but mostly for his children's sake.
He eats and eats and never is avenged.

On Leaving the Inferno

"Then we came forth, to see again the stars."
—Inferno XXXIX:139

"No matter where I fly, I myself am Hell."
—Milton, Paradise Lost

After the wandering in the wood,
After the carnal chasing flesh,
After the wrathful thumping the sullen
After the hell of endless death—
After the fratricides and patricides,
After the river made of blood,
After the agon of the suicides,
After the lustful without love—

After the panderers & flatterers,
The hypocrites & thieves,
The liars & the traitors,
The dead men turned to trees—

They bore the dark inside of them
Back to the world of light again.

PURGATORIO

Postcard from Purgatory #1

> *To course across more kindly waters now*
> *my talent's little vessel lifts her sails,*
> *leaving behind herself a sea so cruel;*
>
> *and what I sing will be that second kingdom,*
> *in which the human soul is cleansed of sin,*
> *becoming worthy of ascent to Heaven.*
> ***—Purgatorio I:1–6***

Dear Mom,

It's fine here, I'm surprised to say.
Much better than I thought it would be.
My room is clean, though the hotel is seedy.
The roaches are small and sleep during the day.
The pool is full of algae and slime,
a thick stew of *goo chartreuse*. Yet I find
swimming in it cures my blues. There's no time
to wallow in guilt and rue. They keep
us busy. Gentle devils cheer as we
fail and try, time & time again, to climb
steep hills of garbage, compost of our sin—
we get to the top and slide down again.
When we run on hot coals, I come in first.
It's no spring picnic, but I've seen worse.

Dante's Song

"If there's no new law that denies
you memory or practice of the songs
of love that used to quiet all my longings,

then may it please you with those songs to solace
my soul somewhat; for–having journeyed here
together with my body–it is weary."

"Love that discourses to me in my mind"
he [Casella] then began to sing–and sang so sweetly
that I still hear that sweetness sound in me.
—Purgatorio II:106–114

There are no poems in Hell. There is no song.
All sounds that soothe the mind forbidden there.
No joy among the damned, no hope their wrongs
might be righted. Beauty cures despair
and beauty cannot live among the lost.
This another price the wicked pay.
A fearful thing to weigh the endless cost
against the pleasures of sin that last a day.

But souls *en route* to God know how to sing.
Their minds have not forgot the ordering
of planets, suns & stars. Music inheres

in the vast universe and all its spheres.
The saved souls cannot help but rejoice
and celebrate the holy human voice.

Dante's Reluctance

"These people pressing in on us are many;
they come beseeching you," the poet said;
"don't stop, but listen as you move ahead."

"O soul who make your way to gladness with
the limbs you had at birth, do stay your steps
awhile," they clamored as they came, "to see

if there is any of us whom you knew,
that you may carry word of him beyond.
Why do you hurry on? Why don't you stop?"
—Purgatorio V:43–51

"Pray for us," they plead, these sorrowing souls,
their bodies left behind, destroyed by murder.
But not before they changed their hearts, repented
of all the evil deeds that they had done.
Pia begged for grace. Heaven heard her.
Buonconte shed a tear. God relented.
The Devil lost what he believed he'd won.
Saved by their prayers, new prayers now their goal
said for them by loved ones who remember.
The weak-limbed little body, the power
of the word—truths Dante learns & laments.

To see how the soul's salvation depends
on others humbling to the stoutest heart,
how small your own attempts, how futile your art.

Virgil in Limbo

"Through every circle of the sorry kingdom"
he answered him, "I journeyed here; a power
from Heaven moved me, and with that, I come.

Not for having–but not having–done,
I lost the sight that you desire, the Sun–
that high sun I was late in recognizing.

There is a place below that only shadows–
not torments–have assigned to sadness; there,
lament is not an outcry, but a sigh."
—Purgatorio VII:23–31

What he did not do his cause for grief.
An eternity of regret.
One long dark night without relief.

Time to brood, never to forget
what he's missing, joy that might have been,
the prize he wants but cannot get.

It seems cruel, given that his sin
is a mild one, considering all.
His error being one of omission,

unlike the one that caused the first Fall,
an act that brought creation to its knees,
that grieves us still and appalls

every living soul, made us unfree,
kills us even down to this day.
Virgil was blind. He just couldn't see

that God was God. He had no way
to know the future. Gripped by the past,
he walked in darkness. Here his sorrows lay,

his place of undoing, his lot cast
with blameless victims of a sad fate.
The first of poets lives among the lost,
cursed by knowledge that arrived too late.

Dante at the Gate

Then he pushed back the panels of the holy
gate, saying "Enter but I warn you–he
who would look back returns–again–outside."

And when the panels of that sacred portal,
which are of massive and resounding metal,
turned in their hinges, then even Tarpeia . . .
did not roar so nor show itself so stubborn.
—Purgatorio IX:130–35, 38

Once you've been through Hell, you're never the same.
It's true for Purgatory—and Heaven, too.
Though you have the same face and same name,

a change has taken place inside of you.
The angel at the gate says as much.
Dante gets it. He is being made new.

His heart has enlarged. His spirit touched
by the suffering souls he has met.
To turn away from any would be such

a sad betrayal of the love that has let
him journey this far. He can't go back
to the man he once was. The wife of Lot

and Eurydice's lover sadly lacked
Dante's resolve—to move forward, never
lamenting his loss, though he be wracked

with sorrow. To persist in his mad endeavor
to find God and her whom he adores,
to be changed and to be changed forever
as he passes through those fateful doors.

Dante among the Envious

I think no man now walks upon the earth
who is so hard that he would not have been
pierced by compassion for what I saw next;

For when I had drawn close enough to see
clearly the way they paid their penalty,
the force of grief pressed tears out of my eyes.

for iron wire pierces and sews up
the lids of all those shades, as untamed hawks
are handled, lest, too restless, they fly off.
—***Purgatorio XIII**:52–57, 70–72*

If thy right eye offends thee, pluck it out.
—***Matthew** 5:39*

Who among us has not loved too much
a thing that's not our own, longed to clutch
some beauty belonging to another?
My sister's new dress, red Mustang my brother
drove to school each day while I rode the bus.
An appetite, a species of lust
woken and whetted by the eye.
To see it is to want it. It's human
nature, the heart quickens to the cry
of desire. What fate more common

than envy of what you cannot possess?

Avoiding sin seems easy if you're blind.

Out of sight, out of mind. You won't obsess.

The soul with his eyes sewn shut is blessed.

Dante & St. Stephen

Next I saw people whom the fire of wrath
had kindled, as they stoned a youth and kept
on shouting loudly to each other: "Kill!"

"Kill!" "Kill!" I saw him now weighted down by
death,
sink to the ground, although his eyes were bent
always on Heaven–they were Heaven's gates–

praying to his high Lord despite the torture,
to pardon those who were his persecutors;
his look was such that it unlocked compassion.
—Purgatorio XV:106–114

The antidote to wrath is always love.
The antidote to fire is always fire.
St. Stephen's passion Dante dreams of

proves this truth. The heart can be a liar,
urging us to rage when gentleness is best.
Though wracked and reviled, saints never tire

of gazing on God. They could not care less
for the stones that strike, the arrows that pierce.
Such martyrdoms are barely a test,

so fixed are they, so full and fierce
their faith in the face of foolish doubt,
forgetful of cost, grateful for grace

that lets them glimpse Heaven in Hell. The shouts
of "Kill!" "Kill!" "Kill!" do not trouble him.
The young man's prayers somehow drown out

their call to murder. That they might learn
to turn their bloodlust into blessing
his fondest wish, that they might burn
with love, even their sins incandescing.

Dante among the Avaricious

"Just as we did not lift our eyes on high
but set our sights on earthly things instead
so justice here impels our eyes toward earth . . .
. . . so justice here
fetters our hands and feet and holds us captive."
—Purgatorio XIX:118–120, 123–124

The pope who speaks knows whereof he speaks.
A lifetime spent with his distorted love
of money blinded him to God. His weak-

ness weighed him down, but did not prove
catastrophic, for he is not in Hell.
The common human passion that drove

his desire somehow curbed, now he tells
Dante of the justness of his torment.
Glued to earth, the greedy are compelled

to stare at what they once were so bent
on having and now view with disgust.
His conversion fully evident,

and yet he is condemned to this. His lust
is cured. Are centuries of punishment
going to make him better? The just-

ice he makes claims for Heaven-sent,
but Dante doubts—at least he seems to.
His gaze compassionate, his knees bent,

he honors this good soul, a man who
blames only himself for his sin,
who begins each tortured day anew
and bides his time until his God forgives him.

Virgil's Fan Club

"On earth my name is still remembered–Statius:
I sang of Thebes and then of great Achilles;
I fell along the way of that last labor.

The sparks that warmed me, the seeds of my ardor,
were from the holy fire–the same that gave
more than a thousand poets light and flame.

I speak of the Aeneid*; when I wrote*
verse, it was mother to me, it was nurse;
my work, without it, would not weigh an ounce."
—Purgatorio XXI:91–99

Statius' words to Virgil a sweet homage
made even sweeter by the charming fact
that he doesn't recognize his master.
Dante flashes a smile, impulsive act
in answer to a fellow poet's love.
Both men find themselves in the presence of
the maker who has made them who they are.
Virgil their hero, Virgil the star
who has guided their minds, brought them this far.
More than a poet, more than a sage,
a human lamp who lights the way to God

as he himself walks in darkness. Awed
by his virtue, lit afire by his flame,
Virgil's disciples praise his name.

Dante among the Gluttons

The branches of another tree, heavy
with fruit, alive with green, appeared to me
nearby, just past a curve where I had turned.

Beneath the tree I saw shades lifting hands
crying I know not what up toward the branches,
like little eager, empty-headed children

who beg–but he of whom they beg does not
reply, but to provoke their longing, he
holds high, and does not hide, the thing they want.
—Purgatorio XXIV:103–111

There is no stronger urge than appetite,
the need to eat embedded in our flesh.
Our love of food so great it's hard to fight
against it. As infants we sense that death
looms as consequence if we do not eat.
And so this is the penance that most haunts
me. The hollow eyes and bony bodies
of the famished, faces flaccid and gaunt
greet Dante and harrow his full heart.
Contrapasso proves to be the art
of cruelty, at times, instead of justice.

The souls suffer for their nature, ravenous
with want, for having fed too well.
Though temporary, it's still a taste of Hell.

Christ in Purgatory

All who die in God's grace and friendship, but still imperfectly purified after death undergo purification. The Church gives the name "Purgatory" to this final purification of the elect, which is entirely different from the punishment of the damned.
***—The Catechism of the Catholic Church** (1030–31)*

Christ knew Purgatory just as well
as He knew Heaven or He knew Hell—
better, in fact, since He knew suffering
as a temporal state, a fleeting thing
that afflicts us briefly, then it's done.
Call it the cost of being human.
Yet Dante can't let Christ journey there.
The place unfit for such as He
who never sinned, who never dared
to disobey his Father, who strived to be
faithful in little and faithful in all.
No task was too great, no task too small
to perform with love, no tear nor sigh,
though He knew, in the end, He'd have to die.

Though He knew in the end He'd have to die,
He performed with love. No tear nor sigh
sullied His tasks, not great nor small.
Faithful in little and faithful in all,
He obeyed his Father, strived to be
free of all sin, even though He dared
visit places unfit for such as He.
Still, Dante won't let Christ journey there,
though He paid the price of being human,
pain that afflicts us and then it's done.
A temporal state, a fleeting thing
is this condition of suffering.
Christ knew Heaven and Christ knew Hell,
and He knew Purgatory just as well.

Virgil's Farewell

Then Virgil set his eyes insistently on me and said:
"My son, you've seen the temporary fire
and the eternal fire; you have reached
the place past which my powers cannot see.

I've brought you here through intellect and art;
from now on, let your pleasure be your guide;
you're past the steep and past the narrow paths.
. . .
Await no further word or sign from me:
your will is free, erect, and whole–to act
against that will would be to err: therefore
I crown and mitre you over yourself."
—Purgatorio XXVII:126–32, 139–42

Teacher to student, father to son,
the poet takes leave of his charge.
Virgil the master, the chosen one.

No burden too heavy, too large
to lift for pilgrim Dante's sake.
His duty he's discharged

with dignity and godly grace.
So back to Limbo he goes,
assumes his left and lowly place

forever. Now life in *Inferno*
is sure to be better somehow.
Forever changed, Virgil will know

his bondage freed Dante. Now
he can savor his willing sacrifice,
remembering when and how

they moved across Hell's lake of ice,
heard the holy souls singing to them
on the road to God and Paradise.

Dante Meets Beatrice

"Dante, though Virgil's leaving you, do not
yet weep, do not weep yet; you'll need your tears
for what another sword must yet inflict."
. . .
"Look here! For I am Beatrice, I am!"
—Purgatorio XXX:55–57, 72

"What's in a name? That which we call a rose
By any other name would smell as sweet."
—Romeo & Juliet, II,ii,43–44

This cannot be what he thought it would be,
the sight of her, at last, so long beloved,
the consummation of what was to be

since his first descent from the world above
to the Hell he had to walk through, his aim
a meeting much imagined and dreamt of.

He stands alone and hears her speak his name,
a word no soul has uttered all this time
as if forgotten. He's not the same

Dante that he was when he set out. The climb
has tired him and tried his pilgrim soul.
He knows that he's no longer in his prime.

But Beatrice will not have it. Her goal
to make her lover better than he was,
to take this broken man and make him whole.

She calls to him, as Christ called Lazarus,
urging him to leave his self-made tomb,
and sets his humble name next to hers.

Dante's heart is full. There seems no room
for love beyond what's already there.
He will learn fast, he will learn soon

the human soul's capacity to care
is endless. Beatrice's love is tough.
His sins confessed, they vanish in the air.
Love can never be too much or enough.

PARADISO

Dante in Heaven

I was within the heaven that receives
more of his light: and I saw things that he
who from that height descends, forgets or can
not speak . . .

Nevertheless, as much as I, within
my mind, could treasure of the holy Kingdom,
shall now become the matter of my song.
—Paradiso I:4–7, 10–12

And now it is you face
another kind of place,
the sight of which will silence
your song. But not yet.
Instead for now you try
to capture sound and sense,
to take us pilgrims with you
as you and Beatrice fly
to Paradise's heights.

You'll try to get it right
and fail, just as you
have many times before.
It's your pluck we adore.
You've given us so much.
And now you give us more.

Dante's Warning

O you who are within your little bark,
eager to listen, following behind
my ship that, singing, crosses to deep seas,

turn back to see your shores again: do not
attempt to sail the seas I sail: you may
by losing sight of me, be left astray.
—Paradiso II:1–6

Is it possible, having come so far,
that you would send us home again? No star
to guide us, no rhyme or meter to speed
us on our way? Arrived, at last, at the gates
of heaven, you tell us we're not fit to follow
you, the bread of angels no fare for us?

Though less-than-learned, we are hungry, too.
Hungry as philosophers. Hungry as you.
In fact, we little ones have greater need
to see the truths our fates have not allowed
us to glimpse through study. Didn't Jesus preach
that only children can even hope to reach
the Paradise you tell us we can't own?
Forget it. We're not leaving you alone.

Dante on the Moon

"But tell me; though you're happy here, do you
desire a higher place in order to
see more and to be still more close to Him?"

Together with her fellow shades she [Piccarda] smiled
at first: then she replied to me with such
gladness, like one who burns with love's first flame:

"Brother, the power of love appeases our
will so–we only long for what we have;
we do not thirst for greater blessedness."
—Paradiso III:64–72

The Heaven of the Moon the strangest place
that Dante has so far seen. What he finds
are souls for whom desire is erased,

an eternal paradise of the mind.
No lust for preferment, no bitter need
for what one cannot have, no wasted time

lamenting what they lack. These souls are freed
from what torments each creature he has met
on the path from the dark wood to here. Greed

has no hold on the hearts of the blessed.
They know neither hunger nor the pain of thirst.
Sins committed are atoned for and confessed.

The lowliest of heaven are uncursed
by the appetite that brought us all to ruin,
the appetite that makes us flawed and human.
Where desire is defeated, love comes first.

Dante the Master Chef

Now, reader, do not leave your bench, but stay
to think on that of which you have foretaste;
you will have much delight before you tire.

I have prepared your fare; now feed yourself,
because that matter of which I am made
the scribe calls all my care unto itself.
—*Paradiso* X:22–27

The feast of the heavenly banquet what Dante
has made for us all. The garlic simmers
in the pan. Olive oil sheens and shimmers.
The tomato sauce bubbles rich and picante.
He tosses linguine with pecorino,
tears up fresh basil and folds it in.
If cooking were music, this is andante,
the slow release of the flavor of sin

redeemed by the grace of his holy art.
What poem more delicious than *Paradiso*?
Food for the soul and food for the heart.
The table is set—he gathers us in.
He promises more, an endless repast.
The only true joy is joy that lasts.

Dante among the Blessed Souls

One and the other choir seemed to me
so quick and keen to say "Amen" that they
showed clearly how they longed for their dead bodies–

not only for themselves, perhaps, but for
their mothers, fathers, and for others dear
to them before they were eternal flames.
—Paradiso XIV:61–66

To think there's no desire in Heaven's wrong.
Though Dante sees the spirits' joyful dance,
and hears them raise their voices in glad song,

he also learns they're savoring the chance
to enter their loved bodies once again.
To take on flesh and blood a circumstance

they welcome, the promise of resurrection
an end they wish for. To be a flame
less a delight than to be human,

in possession of your face and your name,
those elements that make you who you are,
the only things on earth that you could claim

as your own. Who wants to be a star,
the moon, or the sun when you could be a man
or a woman? What life can compare

with the one we live, the gift that was given
to our first parents, poisoned by death,
but now redeemed and rectified? No sin

or sickness, the chance to draw breath
in a world without passing or pain?
Every human prayer and shibboleth

has conjured this dream. The souls give voice
to our own "Amen," and Dante's, too.
Together all of us rejoice
in the hope of salvation come true.

Christ in Paradise

And here my memory defeats my wit:
Christ's flaming from that cross was such that I
can find no fit similitude for it.

But he who takes his cross and follows Christ
will pardon me again for my omission–
my seeing Christ flash forth undid my force.
—***Paradiso XIV:103–108***

Christ rides high on his cross in Heaven
in Dante's eschatological vision,
a cross of fire and a cross of light
that sears his mind with its beauty and might,
a cross of singing and a cross of song
enchanting his ears. Christ the Risen
who conquers death, Christ the Strong
who takes Dante's breath away, so fine
a figure is He. He takes his time
trying to say what cannot be said.
Words seem worthless as they fall dead
on the page. Still he ransacks his brain,
counting the meter, shaping his lines
where Christ rhymes with Christ, every time.

The Prophecy

"You shall leave everything you love most dearly:
this is the arrow that the bow of exile
shoots first. You are to know the bitter taste

of others' bread, how salt it is, and know
how hard a path it is for one who goes
descending and ascending others' stairs."
—Paradiso XVII:55–60

For a man who weeps so much you amaze me.
It takes courage to ask what the future holds
and more courage to hear it, to look and see

what will become of you as you grow old.
You can't forget, once the words are spoken,
though your knees may knock, your blood run cold.

Hope for a happy life will be broken
as you listen to your luckless fate unfold.
Your fortune-teller's eloquence a token

of love for you, though his speech is bold.
Compassion in his voice, but not pity.
He sees your sorrow but will not withhold

the truth. And so before heaven's Deity
you graciously accept what you now know.
Nothing can destroy your fealty.

You've come so far, and you have far to go.
You'll need God in your corner, by your side,
and all the wisdom you've gained down below

before arriving in this Paradise.
You're armored now, ready for the fight
of your life, bullet-proofed against surprise.
Darkness cannot overpower your light.

Dante Is Asked a Rhetorical Question

"Now who are you to sit upon the bench
to judge events a thousand miles away,
when your own vision spans so brief a space?"
—Paradiso XIX:79–81

Like Job before him, Dante must be schooled.
The ways of God are not for men to know,
or women either. It's human to be fooled

by our own minds as much as by our hearts.
We want a god who will forgive all things.
We practice trespassing like it's a fine art,

love the pleasure of sin but not the sting
of judgment. And yet we understand
punishment for having done something

forbidden. But what about the hapless man
born before the Savior came to save?
Like Virgil and the pagans, they are damned

for eternity, no matter how brave
or good they were all their earthly days.
They are consigned to an everlasting grave.

Dante listens, though the question chafes
the reader. Is it true our sight's so poor?
Is there no love in heaven, no fail-safe
for the soul whose broken heart is pure?

Beatrice's Smile

"Were I to smile, then you would be
like Semele when she was turned to ashes."
—Paradiso XXI:4–6

Poor Semele was not as blessed as Dante.
Her lover did not tell her she would burn.
The splendor of a god, the human fancy
a combination she would have to learn
is deadly by dying. Flesh cannot withstand
the glory of god's grandeur unrestrained.
Dante knows this, and yet he still desires
the fire that first set his flesh aflame
in Florence on that fateful day, aspires
to glimpse her beauty and stay a mortal man,
to not be rendered a cinder, a blanched branch
lightning-struck and withered down to ash.
What Dante wishes, Beatrice cannot give.
Unlike Semele in love, he gets to live.

Dante's Smile

My eyes returned through all the seven spheres
and saw this globe in such a way that I
smiled at its scrawny image.

The little threshing floor
that so incites our savagery was all–
from hills to river mouths–revealed to me.

My eyes then returned again to her fair eyes.
—Paradiso XXII:133–35, 150–54

The astronauts who saw the earth wept.
Hanging in the black of space it shone
like the prize they thought it was. A secret kept

from ordinary men, they saw our home
in all of its blue beauty and its charm,
truth they guessed but hadn't fully known.

But Dante saw it clearer, saw the harm
we do ourselves and to the ones we love.
He was surprised, utterly disarmed

to see from such a distance, so far above,
the pettiness and violence of our days,
viciousness—by even him—undreamt of.

And from his perch in heaven, in his daze,
he smiled—as the Creator must smile, too—
to see our vanity, the brazen ways

we do the things we're not supposed to do
and still think mercy's what we ought to get.
Though surely Dante's smile is full of rue,

a man who knows remorse and regret
for his own sins. Perhaps that's why he turns
his gaze to Beatrice, though it's unmet,

thus to let her know what he has learned—
that folly is the rule among our kind,
the gift of grace, undeserved and unearned,
the only source of joy we'll ever find.

Dante's Hope

If it should happen . . . If this sacred poem–
this work so shared by heaven and by earth
that it has made me lean these long years–

can ever overcome the cruelty
that bars me from the fair fold where I slept
a lamb opposed to wolves that war on it,

by then with other voice, with other fleece,
I shall return as poet and put on,
at my baptismal font, the laurel crown.
—Paradiso XXV:1–9

A poet ought to be allowed to dream.
Though Dante knows of his sad destiny
he cannot help but hope, conjure the scene

of his return to his beloved city.
A hero's welcome awaits him there.
We fellow-pilgrims cannot help but pity

a man who wants so much, who deeply cares
for the love of the people he left behind,
the place where he was baptized, the place where

his life as Holy Poet began. His crime
negligible, the cause of his exile
the fault of others. The passage of time

might mend division, might reconcile
the wolves and lambs so there might be peace.
Dante's hope fantastic, Dante's hope wild

knowing human nature. Evil won't cease
because one wants it to. But hope he will
in the face of reason. His release

the gift that gives his fool heart a thrill,
another heaven, his own paradise.
With fierce devotion, all his poet's skill,
he reckons but can never win the prize.

Dante Loses Beatrice

By now my gaze had taken in the whole
of Paradise–its form in general–
but without looking hard at any part;

and I, my will rekindled, turning toward
my lady, was prepared to ask about
those matters that inclined my mind to doubt.

Where I expected her, another answered:
I thought I should see Beatrice, and saw
an elder dressed like those who are in glory.

"Where is she?" I asked him instantly.
—Paradiso XXXI:52–60, 63

What you expect is never what you get.
A lesson that you clearly haven't learned.
Remember Virgil? Hell? Or did you forget

your shock at every circle, every turn
on your journey from there to Paradise?
The way the frauds froze, the lovers burned,

the angry boiled in their blood. Your eyes
have seen horrors not to be believed.
You met them with your own tears and sighs.

So how is it now when Beatrice leaves
you are amazed? Why is permanent surprise
written on your face? You are deceived

by your hopes. *La speranza* lies.
Be content in knowing good will come.
Though the mind suffers and the body dies,

we are preserved by love. Do not succumb,
Pilgrim Friend, to doubt. You've come so far,
from the sinner you were to who you've become.

You are our hero, conversant with stars,
companion of blessèd saints and souls.
The story you've told you have made ours.
We read and reread it. It never gets old.

The Price of Paradise

What little I recall is to be told,
from this point on, in words more weak than those
of one whose infant tongue still bathes at the breast.
—***Paradiso XXXIII:106–108***

Truly I tell you, unless you change
and become like little children,
you will never enter the kingdom of heaven.
—***Matthew 18:3***

The power of speech the price Dante paid
for a brief fleeting vision of God.
Words his instruments, tools of his trade,
simply vanished. The stunned poet saw
deep mysteries his tongue could not tell.
The fires of purgation, the horrors of Hell
did not rob him as high heaven did.
Lost to himself, he became otherwise,
was rendered young and dumb again.
This is what happens in paradise.
When the soul encounters the Holy One
there is no longer need for a poem.
All you have written becomes mere straw.
An eternity looms of language-less awe.

EPILOGUE(S)

Dante, Darling,

You are the bomb. We all know it, too.
Our hearts belong only to you.
Your starved Ugolino haunts us still
long after the cover is closed
on your dope epic, your killer book.
No Medusa with her killer look
could keep us out of your Heaven or your Hell.
Like Juliet, your Francesca knows
the price of love, the name of the rose
she aches to hold to her aching breast.
Because of you we know the rest
of her story. We, too, know you wept
as you told it, as good Virgil guides
the truest of lovers to Paradise.

Dante's Bargain

Dante gave all he owned
for a piece of Florentine sky.
A star above the firmament,
a blaze that has not died
despite the 700 years
that came and quickly went.
His tale of exile and his tears,
the lifetime that he spent
composing lines, creating rhymes
to make the perfect poem
have all survived the test of time.
No poet's better known.
He earned his fame, he paid the price.
A Dante doesn't happen twice.

Acknowledgments

I am grateful to the editors of the following journals in which some of these poems have appeared or will soon appear:

Alabama Literary Review: "Postcard from Purgatory #1"

America: "Dear Dante," "Dante Among the Suicides," "The Price of Paradise"

Christian Century: "Dante Meets Beatrice"

First Things: "Virgil in Limbo"

Italian Americana: "Dante, Darling"

Italian Poetry Review, in English & Italian translation, translated by Bruno Nacci & Susanna Barsella: "Dear Dante," "Dante Among the Lovers," "Swimming with Dante," "Dante Among the Diviners," "Dante's Warning," "Dante, Darling."

Literary Matters: "The Prophecy"

Living City: "Dante's Smile"

Books don't come out of nowhere; in fact, they often result from multiple sources of inspiration. I'd like to close here with a word of thanks to one of those primary sources, my colleague and friend Susanna Barsella, Fordham University Dante scholar who had the brilliant idea of starting a Dante reading group on our campus nearly a decade ago. "Fordham Reads Dante" has been meeting ever since, bringing together students, faculty, scholars, and Friends of Dante of all stripes. I have been honored and delighted to serve as co-convener of "FRD" and am grateful to the distinguished guests and dedicated group members I have met over the years for my own re-education in All Things Dante. Without Susanna and this ongoing conversation, *Dear Dante* would not exist.

I would also like to thank poet and translator Bruno Nacci, along with Susanna Barsella and Alessandro Polcri, editor of *Italian Poetry Review,* for making a selection of these poems available to readers in Italian, a circumstance I would never have hoped for were it not for their generous willingness to translate and publish the poems. *Grazie, amici!*

I am grateful to sculptor Timothy Schmalz for permission to use the image on the cover of *Dear Dante*. It is one of 100 sculptures he created in celebration of the 700th anniversary of Dante's death, each depicting an action that takes place in the 100 cantos of *The Divine Comedy*. This particular sculpture depicts Canto XXXI of *Purgatorio* wherein the spirit of Mathilde, a companion of Dante's Beloved Beatrice, bathes him in the waters of forgetfulness and forgiveness, washing away his sins in preparation for bringing him into Paradise.

In addition, I am grateful to my colleagues at the Curran Center for American Catholic Studies, past and present, for their support and encouragement in all of my poetic endeavors, especially Maria Terzulli, whose devotion to our work inspires me daily and whose friendship has been a blessing in the nearly two decades we have worked together.

I am grateful to the editors and staff members at Paraclete Press whom I have been fortunate to work with on this book, as well as on previous projects. The dedication, professionalism, and creativity of the Paraclete Dream Team is unparalleled, in this writer's experience. I am grateful for their beautiful mission, for their faith in my work, and for their unfailing support.

Finally, I am grateful to my family and friends for their love and enduring patience with my various projects and writerly obsessions, most of all, my husband Brennan—my Beloved, my partner in the long literary life we have led, and my best reader.

A Note on Translation

The epigraphs from Dante's *Commedia* quoted in this collection are drawn from Allen Mandelbaum's translation of *The Divine Comedy* (New York: Everyman's Library, 1995).

The excerpts used in this book are found on the following pages in Allen Mandelbaum's translation of *The Divine Comedy* (in order of appearance, beginning with the book's epigraph from Dante): 61, 59, 61, 74, 73, 80, 84, 107, 113, 141, 149, 165, 206, 213, 217, 224, 236, 244, 257, 274, 286, 306, 315, 329, 344, 357, 379, 384, 391, 423, 445, 446, 460, 469, 477, 486, 497, 528, 540.

IRON PEN

O that my words were written down!
O that they were inscribed in a book!
O that with an iron pen and with lead
they were engraved on a rock forever!

—Job 19:23–24

Outcast and utterly alone, Job pours out his anguish to his Maker. From the depths of his pain, he reveals a trust in God's goodness that is stronger than his despair, giving humanity some of the most beautiful and poetic verses of all time. Paraclete's Iron Pen imprint is inspired by this spirit of unvarnished honesty and tenacious hope.

OTHER IRON PEN BOOKS

Andalusian Hours, Angela Alaimo O'Donnell

Begin with a Question, Marjorie Maddox

The Consequence of Moonlight, Sofia Starnes

Cornered by the Dark, Harold J. Recinos

Eye of the Beholder, Luci Shaw

Exploring This Terrain, Margaret B. Ingraham

From Shade to Shine, Jill Pelaez Baumgaertner

Glory in the Margins, Nikki Grimes

Idiot Psalms, Scott Cairns

Iona, Kenneth Steven

Litany of Flights, Laura Reece Hogan

Raising the Sparks, Jennifer Wallace

About Paraclete Press

Paraclete Press is the publishing arm of the Cape Cod Benedictine community, the Community of Jesus. Presenting a full expression of Christian belief and practice, we reflect the ecumenical charism of the Community and its dedication to sacred music, the fine arts, and the written word.

SCAN
TO
READ
MORE

www.paracletepress.com

You may also be interested in...

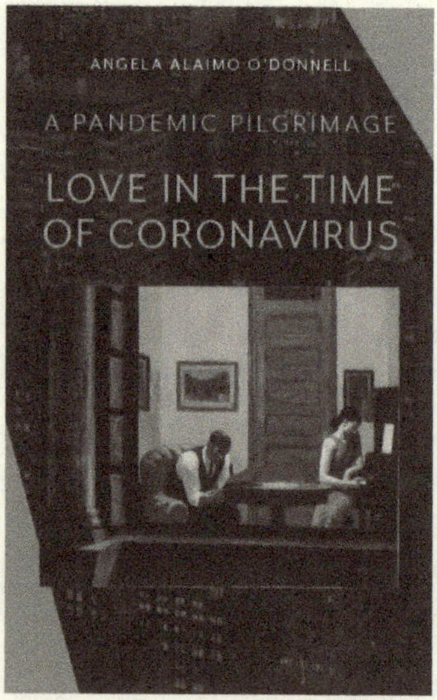